T0295728

THE GULF NATURAL GAS DUAL PRICING REGIME: WTO RULES AND ECONOMIC GROWTH IN THE GULF COOPERATION COUNCIL

ENERGY POLICIES, POLITICS AND PRICES

Additional books in this series can be found on Nova's website under the Series tab.

Additional E-books in this series can be found on Nova's website under the E-books tab.

THE GULF NATURAL GAS DUAL PRICING REGIME: WTO RULES AND ECONOMIC GROWTH IN THE GULF COOPERATION COUNCIL

JUSTIN DARGIN

HARVARD UNIVERSITY-KENNEDY SCHOOL
OF GOVERNMENT
THE DUBAI INITIATIVE

Nova Science Publishers, Inc.
New York

LIBRARY OF CONGRESS CATALOGING-IN-PUBLICATION DATA

The role of energy and development in emerging regions : essays on energy, development and climate change /Editor, Justin Dargin.
p. cm.
Includes index.
ISBN 978-1-61209-775-6 (softcover)
1. Energy policy --Developing countries. 2. Energy industries --Developing countries. 3. Economic development --Developing countries. 4. Environmental policy --Developing countries. I. Dargin, Justin
HD9502.D442 D37 2011
333.7909172/4

2011003799

Published by Nova Science Publishers, Inc. † New York

CONTENTS

PREFACE

Stakeholders in the international economy have long considered energy a crucial aspect of national sovereignty - a commodity inherently political in nature. Because of its contentious nature, energy and natural resources have been the source of conflicts for a millennia. With the sharp increase of the international price of oil and natural gas from 2002-2008, energy subsidization in the energy-rich exporting countries assumed center stage. A narrow focus on this new dynamic, however, obscures the basic issue that developed and developing countries tend to view energy in fundamentally contradictory ways. For developed, OECD countries energy is primarily a tool used to promote the smooth running of the global economy. This new book discusses the role the World Trade Organization and the use of energy as an essential ingredient for modernization in developing regions.

Chapter 1

INTRODUCTION

Stakeholders in the international economy have long considered energy a crucial aspect of national sovereignty-- a commodity inherently political in nature. Because of its contentious nature, energy and natural resources have been the source of conflicts for millennia.

During the early decades of the post-World War Two era, most energy exporting countries were either colonies or protectorates, and energy trade was under the virtually unencumbered domain of the colonial powers. However, this dynamic eventually changed, after the wave of decolonization in the 1960s. While the newly empowered Gulf States found no trade barriers for crude petroleum (unrefined) in Western markets, their downstream petrochemicals and energy-intensive industries (e.g., steel, aluminum etc.) faced stark competition with the often heavily subsidized industries of the developed nations.[1]

With the sharp increase of the international price of oil and natural gas from 2002-2008, energy subsidization in the energy- rich exporting countries assumed center stage. A narrow focus on this new dynamic, however, obscures the basic issue, that developed and developing countries tend to view energy in fundamentally contradictory ways. For developed, OECD countries, energy is primarily a tool to promote the smooth running of the global economy, and therefore, should not be the subject of government interference in terms of price controls or subsidization.

---

[1] This work will use the terms Gulf and Gulf Cooperation Council (GCC) synonymously. The states that make up the GCC are Bahrain, Kuwait, Oman, Saudi Arabia, Oman and Qatar.

In the domestic context, Western countries with an Anglo legal tradition tend to view natural resources, e.g., oil and natural gas, as falling under private ownership rights, guaranteed by the State. In the international sphere, policymakers alternatively view energy as spanning the continuum from transnational investment issues, national security problems, and environmental and geopolitical conundrums.

In terms of host countries, many of whom tend to be developing countries of the global South, the key presumption is that the underground resources of a nation form an integral part, *de facto* and *de jure*, of the national territory in which they are found. From this view, the sovereign disposition of such resources is an inalienable right of national self-determination. It is, therefore, axiomatic that nations driven by this form of commercial nationalism will utilize the legal code to exert control over *their* natural resources.

In developing nations, energy subsidization programs are utilized to promote a host of public policy objectives that have little to do with the tenets of market liberalism. Developing economies tend to consider oil and gas resources as the key to industrialization, and the incubator of sustainable economic growth, therefore, the impetus for many of the Southern developing nations is to leverage these resources into national development and industrialization.

In developing energy-rich countries, the governments (and the populace) view subsidies as social and economic policy instruments that promote a whole range of outcomes, such as developing underdeveloped regions, encouraging particular economic sectors, promoting technical and technological prowess, and providing the base for industrialization.

Energy subsidies comprise two broad sub categories: (1) subsidies of energy inputs to the retail sector (i.e., subsidized disbursement of energy resources such as natural gas, oil, cooking fuels, electricity and coal to the end-user) and the energy-intensive domestic industry, and (2) direct or indirect subsidies (e.g., including below market-pricing of energy inputs) granted to energy industries (e.g., coal, natural gas, and the biofuel industries).[2]

The WTO promulgated rules on subsidies because of their ostensibly trade distorting effect. The Agreement on Subsidies and Countervailing Measures (ASCM) considers a subsidy to exist when there is a financial contribution by a government or a public entity, or where there is domestic price or income

---

[2] Doug Koplow, Ten Most Distortionary Energy Subsidies, The Encyclopedia of Earth (Jan. 26, 2007); For a good analysis of the role of subsidies in the US oil sector, see generally, Doug Koplow and Aaron Martin, Fueling Global Warming: Federal Subsidies to Oil in the United States, Washington, DC: Greenpeace, 1998.

support; such as those considered under GATT Art XVI, or in WTO parlance, comprising a "benefit" that is thereby conferred. Energy-rich exporting countries engage in dual pricing when they administratively set the domestic price of energy inputs to be substantially lower to the retail and industrial sectors than the export price of the same good.[3] The US and EU tend to be against natural gas dual pricing, often alleging that it is either a prohibited subsidy or an actionable, *de facto* specific subsidy under the ASCM.[4]

Existing WTO rules do not adequately cover the energy sector - one of the principal reasons that energy subsidization remains a conundrum under the WTO framework. This is because the rules of the General Agreement on Tariffs and Trade (GATT), which preceded the WTO, were formulated at the end of World War Two, when energy trade liberalization was not a priority. Furthermore, world energy demand was not as high as it is today; consequently, the international prices of oil and natural gas were extremely low.[5] Furthermore, WTO rules involve a distinction between goods and services, even though it is not always clear whether certain energy inputs are "goods" or "services" under WTO classification. For instance, the official WTO classification of electricity is still not quite apparent as to whether it is a good or service, or both, depending on its use.

Additionally, there are distinctions between "trade in natural resources needed to produce energy," which comprises trade in hydrocarbons, and "trade in energy," such as trade in electricity or nuclear energy, which often occurs between two neighboring countries or regions, for example, the pan-Gulf

---

[3] Simonetta Zarrilli, Dual Pricing Practice and WTO Law, Oil, Gas, and Energy Law Intelligence, Vol. 3, Issue 3 (Oct. 2005).

[4] Aldo Spanjer, Russian Gas Price Reform and the EU-Russia Gas Relationship: Incentives, Consequences and European Security of Supply, Energy Policy Volume 35, Issue 5, May 2007, Pages 2889-2898.

[5] As discussed below, there is essentially no international price of natural gas. This is because natural gas has traditionally been a 'stranded resource,' extremely difficult to utilize outside of the immediate area of where it was found. As a result, the natural gas market is fragmented on a global scale, each region (and often jurisdiction) having its own prices. Therefore, there are many different prices of natural gas, depending on the advantage of the negotiating parties, region, etc. In terms of pipelines gas sales, these prices are negotiated between the parties, e.g., Russia and Ukrainian price dispute of 2006, and while there is often a given weight for the international price of oil, the various prices for pipeline-exported gas are quite distinct from region to region. See, generally, Hossein Razavi, Natural Gas Pricing in the Countries of the Middle East and North Africa, The Energy Journal (July 2009). There is an emergent liquefied natural gas "spot" price evolving, however, this is many decades in the future before it has any impact on other natural gas sales. Helena Wisden, The Spot Market Evolves, The LNG Review, 2010 (2010) ; Kenneth Collotta, Uncertain LNG Price Environment turns Focus on Price Revision Clauses, LNG Journal (April 2008).

electrical grid, the Gulf Cooperation Council Interconnection Project.[6] The Gulf countries regulate the cross border exports of electricity as power trading and not trade in energy products. Nonetheless, trade in energy is quite minuscule on a global scale. Conversely, "trade in natural resources needed to produce energy" (particularly trade in oil, gas, coal) is enormous and relates more directly to the traditional GATT/WTO trade in goods. Therefore, energy clearly falls under the ambit of WTO regulations. However, how it is classified, whether as a good or service is consequential as WTO regulations treat goods and services quite differently.

This book will examine the formulation of natural gas dual pricing strategies as official Gulf State policy to spur industrialization and economic modernization. It will consider whether WTO regulations, in particular the Agreement of Subsidies and Countervailing Measures (ASCM), classifies below market pricing as a subsidy, and if it is determined to be a subsidy, whether than subsidy is prohibited or actionable as per the ASCM.

Many Gulf countries supply their domestic industrial sectors with low-cost natural gas in order to spur horizontal and vertical industrial development. Horizontal development occurs when the Gulf governments grant their energy intensive-industries, for example, steel and aluminum smelting, concrete, *et cetera*, below-market pricing for natural gas inputs for power generation, thereby lowering the cost of production several fold. Gulf governments facilitate vertical development when they provide their petrochemical industries low-cost natural gas inputs to produce a variety of products, for example, ethylene, polyethylene, propylene, styrene, for sale on the international market.

In order to diversify economies away from oil and develop broader economic, industrial and social growth, Gulf governments are attempting to transition away from export-oriented petrochemicals production to manufacturing of value-added specialty chemicals for supply to domestic industries that produce, for instance, automotive, appliances and consumer products. One of the reasons that the Gulf countries want to transition away from an export-oriented industrialization (EOI) policy is the dependence of the EOI on demand from the Western economies and their consequent lack of long-term economic stability that would result from a more robust regional demand.

---

[6] Gabrielle Marceau, The WTO in the Emerging Energy Governance Debate, World Trade Report 2010, The World Trade Organization (undated). The Gulf Cooperation Council Interconnection Project is a pan-Gulf electricity grid which spans the entire GCC and connect their national grids to facilitate electricity trading during peak periods.

This book will illustrate that under the ASCM it would be extremely unlikely that a WTO Dispute Panel would find Gulf natural gas dual pricing a subsidy, and if in the unlikely case that it determines so, dual pricing would be neither a prohibited nor an actionable subsidy under the WTO regime.

WTO case law has not yet determined whether dual pricing of natural gas inputs is WTO consistent. Energy-producing countries seeking WTO admission may be obliged to eradicate such programs on the pressure of the Western countries under the accession conditions known as WTO-plus obligations.[7]

This book further argues that not only is natural gas dual pricing in the Gulf region not a prohibited or actionable subsidy, but also it is a vital part of the region's economic and sustainable development.

Chapter Two of the book discusses the concept of sustainable development, defines it, and highlights the link between energy and sustainable development.

Chapter Three considers how the Gulf countries utilize dual pricing of natural gas inputs to foster sustainable development and industrialization, and discusses the historical tension between the Gulf States dual pricing policies and Western countries' energy intensive industries.

Chapter Four posits a general analysis of Gulf dual pricing under the ASCM prongs to test whether such policies fall under the ASCM's subsidy classification.

Chapter Five develops a more nuanced analysis and demonstrates that even if Gulf dual pricing is characterized as a WTO subsidy, it would be neither a prohibited nor an actionable subsidy.

Chapter Six concludes by incorporating the major points of the previous analyses and argues why Gulf dual pricing should not be considered a WTO-inconsistent practice and should rather instead be viewed as a vital element of sustainable development.

---

[7] Julia Ya Qin, WTO-Plus Obligations and Their Implications for the World Trade Organization Legal System, Journal of World Trade, Vol. 37, No. 3, pp. 483-522, 2003.

Chapter 2

THE SUBSIDIZATION OF ENERGY
AND SUSTAINABLE DEVELOPMENT

2.1. WHAT IS SUSTAINABLE DEVELOPMENT?

"Sustainable development" is an elastic term that has not been strictly defined. In its broadest conceptual sense, sustainable development focuses on the equitable development of natural resources for the purposes of fulfilling human needs, in a manner that preserves the ecosystem so that both present and future needs will be met. The 1987 Brundtland Report coined the, perhaps, most widely utilized definition of sustainable development, as "...development that meets the needs of the present without compromising the ability of future generations to meet their needs."[8] In short, it is the rational development of natural resources over the long-term.

Sustainable development requires that the present generation balances the equity of future generations against its needs. Economic growth pursued in a hapless manner has a ruinous impact on the ecosystem, and mitigates the ability for future generations to have high living standards. Taking care of the present needs may also involve balancing the tradeoffs between environmental, social, and economic goals in the short-term. The basic concept here involves the ancient notion of responsible stewardship.

---

[8] United Nations. 1987."Report of the World Commission on Environment and Development." General Assembly Resolution 42/187, 11 December 1987.

2.2. ENERGY AND SUSTAINABILITY

Although oil and gas producing countries do not always judiciously use their resources, and often have myriad, and sometimes, contradictory methods of exploiting their resources, they have all recognized that energy and sustainable economic development are inextricably linked. The lack of access to high quality energy has significant negative effects on a population, leading to increased rates of illiteracy, poverty, gender inequity and environmental degradation.[9] Access to high quality energy helps to meet fundamental human needs such as food production and the provision of health services and assists the development of human capital by enabling the spread of education. Energy is the engine for economic growth and improved living standards. Yet, approximately 1.5 billion people still lack basic access to electricity services, and nearly 2.5 billion rely on traditional biomass as their primary source of energy.[10] Needless to add, energy deficits have an enormous impact on any State attempting to increase productivity and improve the quality of health, life and education.[11]

Under a business as usual scenario, forecasts indicate that these negative statistics will not change significantly.[12] Rajendra Pachauri, the chairman of the Intergovernmental Panel on Climate Change (IPCC), illustrated the structural obstacles that developing countries face in promoting energy access. For example, if rural electrification continues at its current rates in the Indian state of Bihar, it would take approximately 240 years to provide electricity access for the majority of the population.[13]

Certainly, some forms of energy (i.e. hydrocarbons) have led to environmental and climate degradation much more than others, but despite its quite significant externalities, energy is the single most important determinant of economic development and industrialization. Without access to modern electricity and energy systems, many of the UN Millennium Development

---

[9] "Energy as a Compounding Agent: InterIntel and the Democratization of Sustainability." Nuova Energia, February 25, 2009.

[10] Poverty, Energy and Society, The Baker Institute Energy Forum. Available at <http://www.rice.edu/energy/research/povertyandenergy/index.html.

[11] Id. Poverty, Energy and Society, The Baker Institute Energy Forum. Available at <http://www.rice.edu/energy/research/povertyandenergy/index.html.

[12] Id.

[13] Climate Change and Clean Energy Challenges and Opportunities in Addressing Africa's Growing Energy Needs, International Business Forum at World Bank-IMF Annual Meetings (2007).

Goals, specifically the poverty eradication goal, will be extremely difficult to meet. Energy sustainability does not arrive *sui generis*; it is the result of appropriate and well-managed governmental policies and measures, which encompass a wide range of regulatory and market-based interventions.

The Gulf States view fossil fuels as the single most important input factor that will facilitate their economic transformation from primary product exporting countries to advanced, industrialized, manufactured product exporting states. For the Gulf States, energy is the cornerstone for industrialization. Europe's industrial revolution resulted because of the transition from a closed, static agrarian system dependent on natural elements and environmental endowments, to a vibrant, expansionary economy based upon fossil fuels.[14] This lesson was not lost on the Gulf States, as they seek to utilize the dual pricing framework to evolve themselves from dual economies into more integrated, synergistic entities.[15]

2.3. ENERGY SUBSIDIES DEFINED

Energy subsidies have extremely important repercussions for sustainable development by virtue of their impact on the type and quantity of energy consumed. While this text will consider the type of subsidy as defined by the ASCM, the general discussion that follows in chapters 3.0-4.0 will employ a more general and broader meaning.

Energy subsidies, whether to the industrial producer or the end consumer, ultimately lowers the price of the energy input, and thereby raises its demand and overall consumption.[16] Due to its profound impact on the global economy, besides the WTO definition contained in the ACMS discussed in Chapter

---

[14] For the link between industrialization and economic modernization, see John Mathews, Energy Flows and the Process of Industrialization, Copenhagen Business School (June 17-19, 2009).

[15] The concept of the dual economy is attributed to J.H. Boeke from a study of post-war Indonesia. The basic contours of the theory refer to an economy whereby advanced capital-intensive sectors (or enclaves) exist cheek by jowl with poor, traditional labor-intensive sectors. See, generally, Gary Fields, Dual Economy, Cornell University ILR School (2007).

[16] An important distinction must be kept in mind regarding the difference between a consumer subsidy and the "rent" that a consumer receives from utilizing that energy source. A rent is the difference between what the consumer paid for the commodity, and what its value is to him or her. A consumer subsidy lowers the price of the energy input for the end user below its cost of production, and permits greater rent to accrue. (ed) Anja von Moltke, et al, Energy Subsidies: Lessons Learned in Assessing their Impact and Designing Policy Reforms Greenleaf Publishing (Feb. 2004). P.24.

Four, there are a number of various definitions that attempt to explain the notion.

The International Energy Agency (IEA) defines an energy subsidy as any governmental action that primarily concerns the energy sector and lowers the cost of energy production, increases the price received by energy producers or lowers the price paid by energy consumers.[17] Following a similar path, an OECD study defined an energy subsidy, generally, as any measure that maintains prices for consumers below market levels, or prices for producers above market levels – essentially, an official act that reduces costs for consumers and for producers.[18] Neither the IEA nor the OECD definition specifies particular measures as subsidies, even though each establishes broad theoretical boundaries.

The OECD estimates that global energy subsidies approximate nearly $250-300 billion *per annum*, of which fossil fuels subsidization accounts for nearly $200 billion.[19] Energy subsidies elude simple categorization as some have an immediate and direct impact on price, such as tax exemptions and cash disbursements, whereas others have a more indirect influence, for example, regulations that promote a particular fuel or government support of energy research and development. The factors that a government considers in the formulation of a subsidy depend on numerous factors: the subsidization cost on the national budget, the administrative and transaction costs, and the impact on various socio-economic groups.[20]

Energy subsidization tends to be a hidden practice, kept out of the public budget.[21] The opaque nature of energy subsidization is largely because it is politically sensitive. Energy subsidization is such a multifaceted issue because many developing countries discovered during the early days of independence, that their domestic industries and households were unable to afford traditional level of energy consumption at market prices. As a result, they introduced subsidized prices under the view that energy was a public good, and should be

---

[17] Carrots and Sticks: Taxing and Subsidizing Energy, Note of Energy Subsidies and Taxes, The International Energy Agency (Jan. 17, 2006).

[18] (ed) Anja von Moltke, et al, Energy Subsidies: Lessons Learned in Assessing their Impact and Designing Policy Reforms Greenleaf Publishing (Feb. 2004). P.24.

[19] Jean-Marc Burniaux, The Benefits of Eliminating Consumer Subsidies to Fossil Fuels: Results of the OECD-IEA Modeling Exercise, Organization of Economic Co-Operation and Development.

[20] See generally, Leonard Waverman, The Two Price System in Energy: Subsidies Forgotten, Canadian Public Policy / Analyse de Politiques, Vol. 1, No. 1 (Winter, 1975), pp. 76-88

[21] Roland Hwang, Money Down the Pipeline: The Hidden Subsidies to the Oil Industry, Union of Concerned Scientists, 1995.

a central aspect of wealth redistribution. Developing country policymakers also aimed to avoid the negative social implications that significantly higher energy prices would have on the citizenry.[22]

However, not all domestic interest groups support energy subsidization; some groups target energy for its contribution to the national tax burden, and environmentalist groups often allege that rampant energy use and production contributes to environmental degradation. Industry groups frequently jockey for increased governmental support, while foreign interests target domestic subsidies as an unfair competitive advantage. Nonetheless, over the past decade an overall decline in global energy subsidies occurred as nations collectively, moved away from official support of the energy sector, and exposed it to the market forces.[23]

While the global focus on energy subsidization principally concentrates on its trade distortive properties, energy subsidies have numerous externalities with substantial ecological, economic, and social costs that arch beyond the immediate beneficiary of the subsidy. A thorough analysis of the dual pricing of natural gas offers an unparalleled opportunity to explore the nexus between sustainable development and WTO regulations.

WTO members first explicitly discussed energy issues during the 2001 Doha negotiations. The previous rounds, such as Uruguay, did not confront energy in a consistent way.[24] It was the collapse of the Soviet Union in the early 1990s that drove energy-related concerns to become the centerpiece of WTO negotiations.

---

[22] Lev M. Freinkman, et al, Quasi-fiscal activities, hidden government subsidies, and fiscal adjustment in Armenia, Issue 16 of World Bank working paper, World Bank Publications (2003).

[23] While subsidies have fallen in the more traditional energy sectors, e.g., coal, oil and natural gas, subsidization has increased, as of late, in the renewable energy sector. This increased support is predicated upon environmental, and energy-security anxieties, and in certain economically depressed regions, concern with forming a "new economy" based on advanced technology development. There have also been subsidies granted to the agricultural sector to promote the production of biofuels. See generally, Jerry Taylor, et al, Evaluating the Case for Renewable Energy: Is Government Support Warranted?, Cato Institute Policy Analysis, No. 422 (Jan. 10, 2002). A separate category for renewable and environmentally friendly energy technology, and technology that decreases greenhouse-gas emissions, such as carbon capture and storage (CCS) was referred to in the G20 Communiqué as outside of the boundaries of movements towards subsidy reform. The Leaders Statement, The Pittsburgh Summit 2009 (Sept. 24-25, 2009).

[24] The Uruguay Round merely resulted in some members undertaking limited commitments to open their markets to foreign operators in energy services, including field operation of some mining areas and oil and gas fields, pipeline distribution of fuels and services incidental to energy distribution, e.g., gas and electricity. Doha Round Will Benefit Energy Trade-Lamy, WTO News: 20th World Energy Congress, Rome (Nov. 16, 2007).

In the energy arena, dual pricing policies in the transitional economies of the former Eastern Bloc and in the oil-rich countries of the Middle East and North Africa region highlight the importance of balancing the interests of the developmental requirements of industrializing states versus the neoliberalism advanced by the WTO. Developing countries argue that dual pricing is required for their industrialization and economic development, and necessary to provide energy to their impoverished citizenries that cannot afford international market prices.

The founders of the WTO constructed it to promote unfettered trade, in the notion that unencumbered trade leads to global economic growth, lessens wealth disparities between various regions, while furthering comparative advantage.[25] In simplistic terms, a country has a comparative advantage in a good that it sacrifices the least to produce. At the core of the liberal set of economic rules that govern the WTO principles, is the presumption that a country will experience sustainable economic growth from more level competition.

The industrialized countries contend that dual pricing practices are trade distortions that give an unfair competitive edge to the energy-intensive and petrochemical industries of the developing countries, and allow them to export their products to Western markets at prices below that of their Western competitors. The developed countries also allege that dual pricing contributes to environmental pollution and large-scale emissions of greenhouse gases, which the Gulf countries should undertake to significantly mitigate.

From a developing country's view, dual pricing practices are not externally oriented to influence the international market; rather, they are internally oriented to enhance domestic human capital and social welfare. Such adversarial contentions from the developed and developing world exemplify the difficulty that the WTO has with balancing trade equality between various regions.

---

[25] In terms of opportunity cost, this text defines it as the cost of an alternative that must be forgone in order to pursue a certain action. Also, see generally, Steven Suranovic, The Theory of Comparative Advantage—Overview, Int'l Trade Theory and Policy Lecture Notes (1997-2004), http://internationalecon.com/v1.0/ch40/40c000.html. The difference between comparative advantage and absolute advantage is that the latter refers to the ability of a country or region to produce more of a good or service at a lower opportunity cost than its competitors.

Chapter 3

OVERVIEW OF DUAL PRICING
AND SUSTAINABLE DEVELOPMENT:
THE GULF IN FOCUS

As discussed above, dual pricing of natural gas allows a government to provide energy to the retail and industrial sectors below the international market price, and in some circumstances, below the cost of production. Generally, Gulf governments control the price through price control regulation that is an internal administrative price ceiling and floor for energy inputs that direct the maximum or minimum price at which the energy products may be sold domestically.[26]

To be precise, economic literature often characterizes the divergence between the export price and the domestic price as an incurred opportunity cost, rather than as a subsidy. However, trade literature tends to consider the two concepts to be coextensive.[27] While many Western countries conclude that dual pricing of natural gas is detrimental to trade and the environment, governments that engage in the practice deem it essential for industrialization, modernization and a progressive socio-economic agenda.

---

[26] Reforming Energy Subsidies: An Explanatory Summary of the Issues and Challenges in Removing or Modifying Subsidies on Energy that Undermine the Pursuit of Sustainable Development, United Nations Environment Programme, Division of Technology, Industry, and Economics (2002) pp.19-20.

[27] James M. Buchanan (1987). "opportunity cost," The New Palgrave: A Dictionary of Economics, v. 3, pp. 718-21; David Tarr, The Meritis of Dual Pricing of Russian Natural Gas, The World Economy, Vol. 27, No. 8, pp. 1173-1194, August 2004 ; Dual Pricing of Natural Gas Penalises the European Fertilizer Industry with Unacceptable Costs, European Fertilizer Manufactures Association, 2008.

Resource-rich countries attempt to combat the so-called Dutch Disease, and the economic dependency that results from being a mono-resource economy, through strategic diversification into the energy intensive sectors.[28] Allowing the domestic industrial sectors access to inexpensive energy inputs enables a horizontal economic diversification into energy-intensive industries such as cement, lime, glass, fertilizer, non-ferrous metals, plastics and steel. Dual pricing also allows vertical economic diversification along the fossil fuel value chain, and into downstream resource processing such as petrochemicals and refineries.[29]

The most controversial element of such price controls is the below market price set for domestic industrial end-users. By its nature, dual pricing encourages the production of energy-intensive products such as fertilizers, steel and aluminum smelting, *et cetera*. This price control contributes to the substantial price divergence between the prices domestic companies pay for energy inputs, and the prices that foreign firms pay in their home markets. Since domestic industrial end-users may not pay full market price for their energy inputs, there are enormous consequences for the competitiveness of imported products in the domestic markets, and for the global competitiveness of foreign products against those products manufactured from inexpensive energy inputs.

Dual pricing practices also raise significant environmental challenges. The attempt to balance economic development and sustainability often sharpens the conflict between poverty alleviation and environmental protection. However, if used judiciously, dual pricing is a crucial tool for developing countries to promote industrialization, in spite of the potential environmental hazards[30]

Neoliberal economists developed several critiques against dual pricing policies, arguing that it is well-nigh impossible to implement sustainable economic development on a global scale if the developing world consumes

---

[28] The term "Dutch disease" originates from the economic crisis in the Netherlands during the 1960s that resulted from discoveries of vast natural gas deposits in the North Sea. The newfound wealth caused the Dutch currency to appreciate significantly, which resulted in causing exports of all non-oil products to become less competitive on the world market.

[29] Gulf Braces for Huge Petrochemicals Expansion, Emirates Business 24/7 (Apr. 7, 2010).

[30] ome subsidies benefit the environment; for instance, the subsidization of fossil fuels can lead to a net decrease in deforestation in developing countries where the population relies on firewood as primary energy.

energy on the same scale as the developed world.[31] Furthermore, economists who criticize such practices argue that to make natural gas production and economic development even minimally sustainable, energy-rich developing countries should increase domestic natural gas prices to the long-term marginal cost of production level.[32]

If energy conservation is a relatively new concept to the populace, dual pricing policies may lead to enormously wasteful practices in the retail market, and inefficient production practices in the industrial sector.[33] The Gulf region, which has some of the lowest priced natural gas in the world, also has some of the highest demand rates. The rate of natural gas demand in the Gulf is increasing at a rate of 6.6 percent per annum.[34] The low natural gas prices also caused a corresponding growth in electricity demand-most of which is generated by natural gas-and has not encouraged efficient production practices in the industrial sector because of the lack of financial incentive to introduce energy efficiency measures.[35]

The high growth rates caused persistent natural gas shortages throughout the Gulf Cooperation Council (GCC), and affected the respective states' downstream modernization plans. Proponents of dual pricing contend that critics exaggerate the harm of the practice compared to other more perverse energy subsidies, such as direct subsidization of gasoline to consumers in Venezuela and Iran. They also argue that dual pricing may provide a middle way for countries that desire to mitigate the extreme effects of energy subsidization.[36]

---

[31] For a For a detailed study on the ecological repercussions of the increased wealth in the developing world, see, generally, Assessing the Environmental Impacts of Consumption and Production, United Nations Environmental Programme, 2010.

[32] Justin. Dargin, Trouble In Paradise – The Widening Gulf Gas Deficit. Middle East Economic Survey, September 29, 2008.

[33] The Gulf countries in particular are dealing with the issue of inefficient energy usage in the retail sector. See generally, Justin Dargin, " A Model in Preparation for a Post-Oil World" The National (Mar. 20, 2009).

[34] Malini Hariharan, The Middle East is Feeling the Effects of Persistent Natural Gas Shortages, ICIS News (Oct. 7, 2009).

[35] To deal with the growth of energy consumption, many of Gulf countries introduced environmental and energy conservation campaigns. For example, the UAE introduced several campaigns to educate the citizenry about responsible energy usage during the 2000s. See, generally, Simon Aspinall, Environmental Development and Protection in the UAE, United Arab Emirates, a New Perspective, undated.

[36] Dual pricing could be a preferred method of wealth redistribution when compared to direct fuel subsidies. Iran, Yemen, Venezuela and Indonesia are major providers of direct fuel subsidies to their populations. These direct fuel subsidies consume a major portion of their national budgets. Transitioning to dual pricing would be able to mitigate many of the

There are political limits as to what energy-rich states may do to end the practice of dual pricing. Often, strident protests erupt when a developing State attempts to liberalize energy prices. For example, in August of 2005, Yemen doubled fuel prices in a bid to raise government revenue and thereby incited several days of rioting in the process.[37] In Iran, a June 2007 decree to implement fuel rationing in a bid to mitigate the negative effects of the artificially low prices met with demonstrations that included violence, punctuated with anti-government slogans, while gasoline stations were set ablaze.[38] Aware of the dire budgetary straits that resulted from its extensive energy subsidies, the Iranian government promulgated a 2009 bill to reduce-not remove-certain energy related subsidies.[39] The bill, which faced significant opposition from both the Left and Right, languished in Parliament.

The Gulf States discovered that subsidies are particularly difficult to modify politically. Often, Gulf citizens view energy as the part of the national patrimony and the subsidies as part of an implicit social contract, and an essential element of wealth redistribution. However, subsidized electricity and fuel prices have artificially raised consumption. Gulf governments have confronted this issue by introducing demand-side energy efficiency measures, conservation campaigns, and slight electricity price increases to encourage responsible energy usage.[40]

3.1. THE USE OF NATURAL GAS DUAL PRICING TO INDUSTRIALIZE IN THE GULF

Gulf nations have significant interest – and enormous competitive advantages-in the development of petrochemicals as an integral part of their economy.[41] Qatar was the first Gulf country to develop its petrochemical

---

economic distortions and provide low cost energy to more productive enterprises, i.e., energy intensive industries.

[37] Anthony H. Cordesman, et al, The Changing Dynamics of Energy in the Middle East, Volume 2 (Greenwood Publishing Group, 2006).

[38] Petrol Rationing Sparks Riot in Iran, ABC News (June 27, 2007).

[39] Djavad Salehi-Isfahani, Iran: Reform of Energy Subsidies, Monthly Review (Oct. 30, 2009)

[40] The Gulf countries have some of the highest per capita carbon footprints due to the extreme industrialization and high demand rates spurred on by low energy prices. Emmanuelle Landais, UAE Tops World on Per Capita Carbon Footprint, Gulf News (October 30, 2008).

[41] Due to administrative pricing, Gulf petrochemical firms pay approximately; $0.75-1.50 a million BTUs for natural gas feedstock, and Western, i.e. US and EU companies on average

industry with the construction of an ethylene facility at Umm Said in 1974. At the close of the decade, extensive petrochemical facilities were either on-stream or were in the process of being constructed in most Gulf countries. In contrast to other Arab states that sought to shield their economies from the international market in the fifties and sixties through import-substitution industrialization (ISI) policies, the Gulf States realize that as export-oriented economies, access to international markets was essential to continued growth.

As part of their overall economic diversification, Gulf States also sought to leverage their budgetary surpluses into joint ownership stakes in foreign petrochemical enterprises located in the US, China, EU, Turkey, Sri Lanka and Pakistan. The ultimate vision is to thoroughly penetrate the global petrochemical market and achieve not only technology transfer, but also market dominance.[42] By the mid-1980s, the GCC viewed its endeavors at petrochemical expansion as a necessary alternative source of future income, given the precipitous revenue decline due to the mid-1980s oil price collapse.

Gulf nations immensely benefited from the global shift of manufacturing from mature economies to developing regions. By the early 2000s, the GCC became one of the world's major petrochemical producers. To supply the richly percolating BRIC economies - that is, Brazil, Russia, India and China- with petrochemicals, the GCC countries increased the production of ethylene, which is the basic petrochemical in a wide range of plastics and synthetic fibers.

Because of a strong government commitment, geographical proximity to the high-growth Pacific Rim, and low feedstock prices, the GCC became one of the most attractive locations for petrochemical expansion. Primarily because of historically low Gulf gas feedstock prices, generally below $1.50 per Million British Thermal Units (MMBTU), the Western petrochemical industry witnessed a slow migration, in which even well established Western petrochemical firms sought mergers with GCC firms and relocated to the Gulf.

However, not all trading partners view Gulf petrochemical expansion efforts favorably. By 1984, petrochemical exportation became a contentious issue in trade relations between the GCC and the European Economic Community (EEC). In this heated context, the EEC decided to implement tariffs of up to 13.5 percent on Saudi Arabian petrochemical imports that exceeded a certain amount. The EEC also contended that it had been overly

---

pay about $4 per million BTUs. Peter Salisbury, Gulf Petrochemical Producers Maintain Competitive Advantage, MEED, June 26, 2009.

[42] Atif A. Kubursi, Oil, Industrialization and Development in the Arab Gulf States (London: Croom Helm, 1984) p.56.

generous when it designated wealthy GCC nations as "developing countries."[43] Arguing that the European petrochemical industry would collapse, the EEC opposed the GCC request to raise petrochemical import quotas.[44] The GCC argued that the European position was inequitable, not least of all because European exports to the Gulf have historically been subject to minimal duties.

Certainly uppermost on the minds of most GCC officials was the historical knowledge that access to inexpensive Gulf energy resources had for decades been the backbone of the Western Europe's post-World War II economic resurgence. Nonetheless, even after his European tour, GCC Secretary General Abdullah Bishara's attempt to convince the EEC to revise its tariff schedule downwards for Gulf petrochemicals received nothing more substantive than the EEC's restatement of its position. The lack of a resolution prompted the UAE daily, *al-Khalij* to demand that the GCC confront the alleged EEC's intransigence. The GCC, in response to the EEC's tariff, contemplated a trade war -an imposition of a 20% tariff on all European goods that local industry could produce.[45]

More recently, during the WTO accession proceedings, the European Union continued to contend that Saudi natural gas dual pricing grants an unfair competitive advantage to Saudi industry that, in effect, amounted to a subsidy. Both parties signed the final accession agreement on November 11, 2005, with no firm agreement on the reformation of the dual pricing system. The WTO press release announced, slightly ambiguously, that Saudi Arabia's obligations included an agreement that "Saudi Arabia will ensure that its producers and distributors of natural gas liquids (NGL) will operate on the basis of normal commercial considerations, based on the full recovery of costs and a reasonable profit."[46]

Saudi petrochemical production and export promises to be a contentious issue for the near future, since Saudi WTO membership will provide benefits and challenges for its burgeoning diversification strategy. Overall, Saudi Arabia believes that its membership will further enhance the competitive advantages of its petrochemical industries in the international market.

[43] Dore Gold, "The Gulf States" in (ed) Colin Legum, et al, Middle East contemporary survey (The Moshe Dayan Center, 1987) p.385.
[44] Id.
[45] Id.
[46] Anthony H. Cordesman, et al, The Changing Dynamics of Energy in the Middle East, Volume 2 (Greenwood Publishing Group, 2006) p.392.

The WTO enforces a global system of rules that obligate industrialized countries-where energy and petrochemical demand is greatest-to adhere to their bound tariffs: a principle that Gulf countries deem favorable to their export-led development. WTO membership should prove to be an overall advantage for the GCC nations, even though some domestic industries may not be able to compete with Western firms. The unprecedented access that GCC petrochemical products would have in the mammoth markets of the EU, US and Japan would allow a substantial surge in Gulf petrochemical exports.[47]

The GCC's dual pricing practices of natural gas is likely to incite fierce resistance from Western petrochemical firms, who will likely apply pressure to their respective governments to bring a suit in the WTO to halt these practices as an alleged unfair trade practice. Alleged petrochemical subsidies have been a significant obstacle in free trade negotiations between the EU and GCC. Many European policymakers contend that GCC petrochemical firms have an unfair advantage over EU producers because of the low administrative price of Gulf oil and natural gas inputs. EU policymakers claim the low priced natural gas inputs are the result of government subsidies.[48] They claim that the dual pricing makes GCC goods artificially competitive against EU products. Western petrochemical producers argue that Gulf countries contravene WTO rules when they grant an advantage to the domestic petrochemical firms by providing low cost natural gas as feedstock.

Dual pricing concerns have sparked many trade disputes and generated fears of a nascent trade war between the GCC and its largest Western and Asian consumers. In October 2009, the Gulf Petrochemicals and Chemicals Association (GPCA) investigated the viability of a GCC ban on EU, China, and India petrochemical imports in retaliation for their imposition of high tariff anti-dumping measures on GCC petrochemicals. The GPCA Secretary-General, Abdulwahab Al Sadoun, claimed that these anti-dumping measures contravene WTO regulations and announced that, "The GCC industry and our governments will not accept the application of anti-dumping regulations against exports of petrochemicals and chemicals from the Gulf. We have seen a surge in protectionist actions brought by countries to block imports. These cases are baseless and violate international rules."[49]

---

[47] Currently, the Gulf accounts for about 11 percent of petrochemical production, but industry leaders predict that Gulf petrochemicals will capture nearly 20 percent of global production by the next decade. Sean Cronin, Gulf Chemical Firms Eye Growth, The National (Dec. 7, 2009).

[48] Tom Arnold, EU Plastics Tariffs Stoke Concern, The National (June 2, 2010).

[49] Shasshank Shekhar, GPCA Lobbies to Stop Imports of Petrochemicals, Emirates Business 24/7 (Oct. 13, 2009).

In an escalation of the simmering dispute, in June 2010, the EU imposed new tariffs on the UAE, Iran, and Pakistan for petrochemicals utilized in plastic bottles and films. The EU alleged that petrochemical firms from these countries materially damaged EU petrochemical firms by their alleged subsidies and price undercutting.[50] The GCC countries argued that since most natural gas production is from associated oil wells, i.e., natural gas and oil produced together, it thereby results in an extremely low production cost and is a competitive advantage.[51]

As inexpensive GCC petrochemicals inundate Western markets, EU and US petrochemical firms will likely put pressure on their respective governments to present this contentious issue for WTO resolution. When the WTO negotiates comprehensive rules for below market pricing, the GCC would most likely negotiate as a collective bloc to secure the most advantageous outcome.

---

[50] The duties imposed last for four to six months and may be extended for up to five years. They are as high as €142.97 a tonne. Tom Arnold, EU Plastics Tariffs Stoke Concern, The National (June 2, 2010).

[51] Saudi Petrochemicals Sector: Current Situation and Future Prospects, Samba Report Series (August 2009) p.8.

Chapter 4

GENERAL ANALYSIS OF GULF DUAL PRICING UNDER THE SUBSIDIES AND COUNTERVAILING MEASURES AGREEMENT

Under the ASCM, the WTO determines that a subsidy exists when three fundamental elements are present: (i) a financial contribution (ii) by a government or any public body within the territory of a Member, (iii) which confers a benefit.[52]

Questions as to whether the GCC's dual pricing practices are WTO consistent have become increasingly important during the WTO accession negotiations. Even though dual pricing will probably not be found to violate WTO regulations because it fails to meet the three-prong test of the ASCM, the issue highlights the quandaries that the WTO faces in its attempt to discipline these practices.

While the WTO incorporates a myriad of agreements that deal with trade-distorting practices, the ASCM is the one most relevant to the dual pricing issue, as it pertains to subsidies and monitors the actions that a country can take to impose countervailing duties on those alleged subsidies.

In *Brazil Aircraft*, the WTO Appellate Body concluded that financial contribution and benefit are separate legal elements, which when taken together, determine whether a subsidy is present.[53] The Dispute Settlement Body, in *United States-Measures Treating Export Restraints as Subsidies* (*US-Export Restraints*), reasoned that a financial contribution requirement was created to

---

[52] SCM Agreement, Article 1.

[53] Appellate Body Report, Brazil-Export Financing Programme for Aircraft, WT/DS46/AB/R, adopted August 20, 1999, para. 157.

ensure that not all governmental actions that conferred benefits would be classified as subsidies.[54]

The ASCM was negotiated in the late 1980s, when the world's major developed nations embraced free market reform, with its twin pillars of privatization and liberalization. However, emboldened by the global economic crisis, critics contended that the ASCM was outmoded. Some observers would argue that the economic resuscitation efforts of Western governments to save their banking and heavy manufacturing industries have starkly illustrated the inadequacies of the ASCM. Some quarters have called for the ASCM to be modified to include an "escape clause" that would allow countries to adopt limited subsidies in the face of an economic crisis.[55]

Furthermore, some economists have vocalized their criticism of the ASCM, on grounds that it reduces, and nearly eliminates, one of the main pillars of Ricardian liberal economic theory- natural resource comparative advantage.[56] Since the ASCM, under certain delineated circumstances, disallows governments from utilizing their natural resources at favorable rates to their domestic industry, many of these heterodox economists, such as Ha-Joon Chang, argue that the very policies that the developed economies utilized to industrialize are now prohibited by the ASCM.[57]

4.1. THE GENERAL STANDARD OF FINANCIAL CONTRIBUTION UNDER ARTICLE 1.1(A) (1)

The ASCM represents a rather limited notion of a subsidy when compared to the broad conception as discussed in chapter two above. [58]Fundamentally,

---

[54] Panel Report, WT/DS194//R, adopted on June 29, 2001, paragraphs 8.65-8.69.

[55] Marita Wiggerthale, Safeguard Instruments within the WTO- A Development Policy Analysis, Fairer Agrarhandel, 2004.

[56] See generally, Erik Reinert, How Rich Countries Got Rich and...Why Poor Countries Stay Poor, Constable Jan. 25, 2007; Erik Reinert, Increasing Poverty in a Globalized World: Marshall Plans and Morgenthau Plans as Mechanisms of Polarisation of World Economies, The Other Canon Foundation (no date).

[57] See generally, Ha-Joon Chang, Kicking away the ladder: Development Strategy in Historical Perspective, Anthem Press, 2002.

[58] The ASCM incorporated the concept of "financial contribution" after long and drawn-out negotiations. A faction of the delegates argued that that no subsidy existed unless there had been a charge on the public treasury. Other members developed a more expansive concept and concluded that certain types of government intervention did not necessarily take the form of a public expense, but nonetheless distorted trade. World Trade Organization Homepage:

the ASCM contends that, in order to be considered a financial contribution, the governmental action would encompass, at a minimum, such disbursements as grants, loans, equity infusions, loan guarantees, fiscal incentives, the provision of goods or services, and the purchase of goods.[59] An additional condition declares that for a financial contribution to represent a subsidy, it must be "by or at the direction of a government or any public body within the territory of a Member."[60]

The ASCM does not merely limit itself to the official actions of a government, but also includes those actions of sub-national governments and public bodies such as state-owned enterprises and national oil companies (NOCs).

For the purposes of this analysis, the Gulf dual pricing framework may be analyzed under the most relevant sub headings of items (iii) or (iv) of sub-paragraph 1.1(a)(1) of Article One.

Provision (iii) states that a subsidy exists if: a government provides goods or services other than general infrastructure, or purchases goods.

In the GCC, the NOCs most often grant natural gas to industrial users and public utilities. Article 1.1(a)(1)(iii) includes, as subsidies, not just grants of goods or services from the *government*, but also from any *public body within the territory of a Member*. Natural gas could be included under the "goods or services" provision of Art. 1.1(a)(iii). Furthermore, all NOCs in the Gulf may be considered "public bodies" by virtue of this definition, as they are wholly or majority-owned by the government, and under the direct control of either the respective oil ministries or some governmental agency.[61] As Gulf-based NOCs sell natural gas to domestic utilities and the industrial sector, it would meet this threshold. In short, natural gas dual pricing as provided by the NOCs meet the elements of "financial contribution" by a "government or any public body within the territory of a Member."

Subsidies and Countervailing Measures: Overview. Available at < http://www.wto.org/ english/tratop_E/scm_e/subs_e.htm >.

[59] Id.

[60] Id.

[61] See generally, Eric Thompson, Major Oil Companies Operating in the Gulf Region, Petroleum Archives Project: Arabian Peninsula and Gulf Studies Program, University of Virginia. Available at < http://www.virginia.edu/igpr/APAG/apagoilcompany.html>; Valerie Marcel, et al, Oil Titans , Brookings Institute (April 2006).

4.1.1. The Financial Contributions by a Private Entity Standard of Article 1.1(A)(IV)

The ASCM does not govern contributions from private entities unless the private body was entrusted or directed by the government to disburse the financial contribution. This part of the analysis will analyze whether the privately held and joint venture (JV) natural gas companies that supply gas in the Gulf fall under this provision.

In *US-Export Restraints*, Canada alleged that US law and regulations, in violation of the WTO, classified restraints on exports of input products a subsidy in the manufacture of downstream products and, therefore, a violation of the ASCM. The *US-Export Restraints* Panel wrestled with the meaning of the ASCM's use of the term "entrustment" or "direction" in Article 1.1(a)1(iv).[62] The Panel held that the governmental action must be: 1) an explicit and affirmative act, whether through command or delegation; 2) addressed to a particular party; 3) and the object of which is a particular duty.[63] In short, each of these criteria must be satisfied to fulfill the definitional standard of either "entrustment" or "direction."[64] Additionally, the Panel held that the last two elements derive their importance from the first— e.g., an explicit and affirmative action of delegation or command.[65] Of importance to the Gulf dual pricing, the Panel held that export restraints did not meet the "definitional threshold" of financial contribution.

With regard to the JV oil and gas companies, oil and gas field services companies, and public and private partnerships in the Gulf, an explicit and affirmative act of delegation or command is essential to form the governmental nexus. Dual pricing constitutes governmental action, since the Gulf governments "entrust and direct" their NOCs, the IOCs and JVs to provide a certain amount of natural gas to the domestic market at administratively set prices. In *US-Export Restraints,* the phrase, "entrusts or directs" does not necessitate that the delegation or command be promulgated in an official legislative act. An act need only be an operational or a managerial directive to meet the standard.

---

[62] Panel Report on United States — Measures treating exports restraints as subsidies (US Export Restraints) — "Complaint by Canada" (DS194/R) para. 8.29-8.30; See generally, Henrik Horn, et al, The WTO Case Law of 2001, Cambridge University Press of 2001. pp.201-18.

[63] Id. US Export Restraints, at para. 8.25.

[64] Id.

[65] Id. at para. 8.29

Hence, a "public body" as maintained by the ASCM, not only refers to a *de jure* public company but also to a *de facto* public entity that adheres to government dictates and does not follow pure commercial logic. In the Gulf, even the JVs that have been set up to explore, produce or process natural gas, for example, the Ras Laffan LNG Company Limited, formed between Exxon Mobil (30 percent) and Qatar Petroleum (70 percent), produce under the directives of the central authority.

Sometimes the "control test" presents difficulties if the government controls less than 50 percent of all outstanding shares, in which instance it would be necessary to analyze whether the number of shares directly or indirectly held by the government vest operational control to it. However, questions as to whether the respective Gulf States control all of the companies operating in their territories are essentially mute. They have majority control of all JVs, and even direct the exploration efforts of the privately held international oil companies operating on their territory. As exemplified during the 1973 oil embargo, the Arab oil producing countries directed all of the foreign IOCs operating in their territory to pump less oil, and to refrain from the export of petroleum to the embargoed states.[66]

Furthermore, in reference to the control test, the Gulf nations implement dual pricing as a type of administrative process, whereby the government administratively sets the price and directs all of its organs to oversee the purchase and sale of natural gas at this benchmark, whether by NOCs or IOCs operating within its territory.

A second important question is whether Gulf governments direct energy companies operating in the Gulf "provide" natural gas to the domestic market. In *United States-Final Countervailing Duty Determination with Respect to Certain Softwood Lumber from Canada* (*US-Softwood Lumber IV*), the Appellate Body rejected the Canadian argument that "to provide" has a higher definitional threshold than to merely "put at the disposal of" or "make available." Rather, the tribunal found that these words merely refer to the positive act of "giving."[67]

The Appellate Body determined that the Canadian timber program, which recognized certain harvesting rights granted by Canadian provincial

---

[66] However, it was often alleged that the international oil companies did their utmost to only follow the spirit and not the letter of the directives. Mary Ann Tetreault, "Hydrocarbon Production as a Route to Economic Health" in (ed) Leonard Binder, Rebuilding Devastated Economies of the Middle East, Macmillan 2007

[67] United States-Final Countervailing Duty Determination with Respect to Certain Softwood Lumber from Canada (US-Softwood Lumber IV)

governments for loggers to cut timber on government land, was "making available" timber to Canadian harvesters. The tribunal found that this affirmative act of "making available" met the threshold of "providing" under the ASCM Agreement.[68]

There is no dispute that the respective Gulf authorities, not only provide gas directly to certain strategic industries, they also set prices through their normal administrative functions. The act of setting the prices, and directing the NOCs, IOCs and JVs to provide natural gas to the domestic economy at that price is essentially the same as making gas "available," analogous to the *Softwood Lumber* determination, to domestic end users at a specified price

Furthermore, when considering the global energy sector, natural resource regimes differ quite widely. On the extreme end of the continuum, all energy related activity falls under the purview of the State. Yet, on the other end of the spectrum, which is more consistent with Anglo-American legal heritage, oil and natural gas reserves belong to those under whose property it lies. For most resource-rich countries, energy reserves are a strategic sector, and the governments control the commanding economic heights.

Therefore, energy exploration, production, and processing could be an activity "normally" vested in the government or entities directed or managed by the government, for example, joint ventures or oil and gas field services companies. Making natural gas available to the industrial, retail, and power sectors is a practice that is normally followed by governments in the meaning of Article 1.1(a)(1)(iv).

Based on the above analysis, the dual pricing regime in the Gulf fulfills sufficient criteria under either Article 1.1(a)(1)(iii) or under Article 1.1(a)(1)(iv) of the ASCM, to constitute a "financial contribution" under Article 1.1(a)(1), irrespective of the fact whether the natural gas is provided by government-run NOCs or government directed JVs, and privately-held companies.[69]

4.2. INCOME AND PRICE SUPPORT

Article 1.1(a)(2) of the ASCM provides that, apart from a governmental financial contribution, as given under Article 1.1(a)(1), "any form of income or

---

[68] Id.

[69] Justin Dargin, Trouble In Paradise – The Widening Gulf Gas Deficit. Middle East Economic Survey, September 29, 2008.

price support in the sense of Article XVI of GATT 1994," which confers a benefit, represents a subsidy. Income and price supports have important functions in most commodity exporting countries. A representative example of a price support mechanism involves a government purchase of goods from its own national producers at above the international market price, to enhance the profit or revenue that those national producers receive from those goods.[70]

Income support could also occur, if a government were to pay a producer the difference between the actual revenue and a price target.[71] The provision for triggering income or price support proceedings requires an applied cost against the governmental budget.[72] An attempt to prove that price or income support occurred without the representative "public charge (or cost)," is extremely difficult. However, unless the government incurred a charge or a cost, this allegation tends to conflate subsidies with other forms of governmental involvement in the economy, whether it was financial or regulatory, for example, carbon emissions mitigation regulations.[73]

The GATT Analytical Index, which catalogues WTO jurisprudence, defines price and income as relating only to primary products; however, it did not enumerate natural gas. Regardless, it is likely that the drafters would include natural gas in their concept of "primary products." Article XVI of the GATT concerns itself with the prospect that countries promote "price of income support" by elevating domestic prices or ensuring a certain level of producers' income.

By subsidizing domestic producers, who potentially are able to export their products at a lower price, the government enables them to be more competitive in gaining increased market shares.[74] The GATT Members incorporated this core premise into the ASCM, not only to mitigate such activities in the primary product sector, but also to expand the definition of subsidy to incorporate value-added manufactured products.

While the Gulf's natural gas dual pricing framework neither provides price support nor upholds a certain level producer income, it does, at least, have the result, whether intended or not, of ensuring that the prices of petrochemical and industrial products do not drop below a certain level. The

---

[70] Clive Stanbrock, et al, Dumping and subsidies, Kluwer Law International (1996) p.88.

[71] Id.

[72] Pietro Poretti, Regulation of Subsidies Within the General Agreement on Trade in Services of the Wto, Kluwer Law International, 2009 p. 105.

[73] Id. p.107.

[74] Another concern is that the subsidization of domestic producers leads to overproduction in the national market and potentially, lower world prices.

Gulf States did not develop the dual pricing regime with a pricing or income support strategy in mind, and its effect only applies in an indirect way to price ceilings and floors in the downstream petrochemical sector.

Because Gulf natural gas dual pricing fails to meet this threshold of Article XVI of the GATT, it constitutes neither income nor price support under Article 1.1(a)(2).

4.3. A BENEFIT IS CONFERRED

Under the ASCM, neither financial contributions nor income or price support is synonymous with a "benefit." Even though the previous analyses weighed the actions of the donor, questions as to whether a benefit was conferred consider facts from the vantage point of the recipient. Under the ASCM, a benefit is only conferred if the recipient obtained an advantage that it would not have had in a normally functioning market. In short, the effort to determine whether a benefit were conferred, is essentially a "but for" test. WTO case law has struggled to properly ascertain what is a "benefit," since the ASCM does not define when a benefit has been conferred.

Many WTO panels have utilized the "private investor test" to distinguish those cases in which the government grants an ostensible benefit, such as an equity infusion or a financial contribution, to a company, from cases where it has not. The crux of the private investor test is that an operator who obtains from the government what it could not receive from the market, has received a benefit, within the meaning of Art. 1.2 Of the ASCM.

On the other hand, WTO Panels have sometimes relied on the production cost as a benchmark to determine whether a benefit has been conferred.[75] In *Canada-Measures Affecting the Export of Civilian Aircraft* (Canada-Aircraft), the Appellate Body held that the word "benefit" used in Article 1.1(b) implies some type of comparison. According to the Appellate Body, a "benefit" arises under the Article 14 guidelines if a recipient has received a "financial contribution" on terms more favorable than those available to the recipient in the open market.[76] Article 14 of the ASCM involves the calculation of the subsidy's value, relative to the benefit to the recipient. This provision clarifies

---

[75] This more constrained definition has not been widely used, but it had a central role in Canada-Measures Affecting the Importation of Milk and the Exportation of Dairy Products, Dispute DS103 and European Community-Export Subsidies on Sugar.

the meaning of the term "benefit" in Article 1.1 (b) of the ASCM.[77] Article 14 states that "benefit" references the benefit to the recipient, and that the market or private investors are the relevant benchmarks. Article 14(d) essentially holds (1) that to confer a benefit, a good has to be supplied at "less than adequate remuneration," and (2) that the adequacy of the remuneration must be determined "in relation to prevailing market conditions in the country of provision."

To determine if Gulf gas producers "confer a benefit" through their natural gas dual pricing system, the test must consider whether the involved Gulf gas distributors provide gas at a less than adequate remuneration, as set forth in Article 14(d). The Gulf countries administratively set the price of natural gas in a range of $.90-1.40 per MMBTU. On the other hand, the international gas sales price for liquefied natural gas (LNG), in a typical contract from Qatar, hovers at approximately $8 per MMBTU.[78]

This differential is misleading, however. A problem with using Qatari LNG sales prices as a benchmark is that it is contractually developed, rather than set by the market. Unlike oil, natural gas has no global price. In fact, the natural gas market is segmented and prices are widely divergent in all of the major gas exporting countries, Russia, Qatar, Indonesia, *et cetera*. These wide differences in scale stem from the inherent qualities of natural gas. These differences are also due to the fact that natural gas has been, at least until the relatively recent advent of LNG technology, a 'stranded resource.'

Traditionally, if natural gas fields were far from utilization areas (e.g., industrial areas), it was practically unexploitable. This situation is changing, as more natural gas is converted to LNG and the nascent LNG spot market develops apace.[79] As increasing numbers of countries become LNG users, and construct re-gasification plants, and the number of LNG tankers increases, it is easier for spot cargoes to reach new markets. A truly global price for natural gas in the form of LNG would then develop, but as of yet, an international price does not exist. In terms of pipelines, there is no recognized international

---

[76] Canada-Measures Affecting the Export of Civilian Aircraft, Report of the Appellate Body, WT/DS70/AB/R, 2 August 1999 at para. 157-58.

[77] During the Doha Round, it has been suggested that a reference to the market benchmark should be contained within Article One itself.

[78] Dinakar Sethuraman, Global LNG Supply to Exceed Demand in 2010, Bernstein Says. Bloomberg News (Nov. 23, 2009).

[79] Julia Hayley, Analysis-LNG Spot Market Growing, But Faces Hurdles, Reuters (Apr. 26, 2007).

price for transnational gas; the exporting and importing nations have complex negotiations to develop the price of exported gas via pipeline.[80]

In *US-Softwood Lumber IV*, the Panel and Appellate Body dealt with a comparable state of affairs. The Canadian provincial authorities were the majority suppliers of stumpage and the private market was undersized. The Appellate Body held that, under Article 14(d), private prices in the market of the provider would generally embody a sufficient standard of the adequacy of remuneration for the supply of goods, and that these private prices were to be the primary benchmark for the remuneration analysis.[81] However, the Appellate Body held that Article 14(d) did not mandate analyses based on private prices in the supplier's local market in every situation.[82]

The Appellate Body found that price distortion could result in the local market because of the government's overwhelming presence as the provider of first resort. In such situations, the Appellate Body found that it would not be plausible to calculate a benefit predicated solely on private prices, and that the investigating authorities must have recourse to benchmarks besides domestic private prices.[83]

The Appellate Body also held that, an assertion that a government is a predominant force in the supply chain would not, *ipso facto*, show that the market price is distorted; rather, each case is to be approached on its individual merits. *US-Softwood Lumber IV,* however, does bear on dual pricing in the Gulf, as the Gulf governments are the major, if not the sole, gas supplier in the domestic market. Moreover, the domestic price of natural gas is set administratively, therefore, whatever private suppliers of gas there are, for example, Crescent Petroleum (UAE), Mubadala (UAE*) et cetera*, receive pricing signals directly from the respective governments.

US-Softwood Lumber IV developed a system of alternative benchmarks to determine adequate remuneration for application to situations that involve market distortion. The benchmark utilized must be intrinsically connected with

[80] For an analysis of pipeline pricing in the Mediterranean basin, see, Mark Hayes, The Transmed and Maghreb Projects in Natural Gas and Geopolitics from 1970-2040 (ed) Amy Jaffe, et al, Cambridge University Press, 2006 pp.64-88; For a concise explanation of the Russian pipeline gas pricing strategy in Europe; see, Andrew Kramer, Russia to Europe with a Natural Gas Pipeline, New York Times, Dec. 10, 2005; In terms of natural gas pricing frameworks in the Middle East and Central Asia, see Turkey, Azerbaijan Agree on Natural Gas Price, World Bulletin, February 4, 2010.

[81] Appellate Body Report, US-Softwood Lumber IV, paras. 90, 96.

[82] Id.

[83] Paras. 101, 103

the "market conditions in the country of provision."[84] The Appellate Body found that the provision for goods or services should not be considered as conferring a benefit unless the provision is made for less than adequate remuneration, or the purchase is made for more than adequate remuneration. According to the *Softwood Lumber IV* Appellate Body's interpretation of Article 14, it found that the adequacy of remuneration is determined in relation to prevailing market conditions for the good-in this case natural gas- in the country of provision or purchase (including price, quality, availability, marketability transportation and other conditions of purchase or sale).[85]

The *Softwood* Appellate Body held that prices of similar goods sold by private suppliers in the country of provision are the primary benchmark; this methodology should not be followed if the government's predominant role as supplier in the economy is found to have a distortive effect. If such a distortion is positively established, not merely presumed, then the alternative methodology to determine the adequacy of remuneration are proxies that weigh the price for similar goods on the world market or a methodology based on production costs.

By utilizing the above analysis in relation to the Gulf countries, a predominant role for the government in the natural gas sector is evident. The Gulf governments do not allow majority equity holdings for foreign energy companies in natural gas fields, and the Gulf governments direct the production rates and prices to which energy companies operating in the jurisdiction must adhere. Therefore, domestic natural gas prices would not be the benchmark to use in determination of whether there has been adequate remuneration, and one of the other two methodologies must be used.

---

[84] US-Softwood Lumber IV, para. 84 (WT/DS257/AB/R)

[85] Although not yet adopted, the US and EU, concluding that the Softwood Lumber dispute decisions were in their favor, proposed a revision to the ASCM during the Doha Round. The two stakeholders promoted the view that a subsidy may exist under the draft text if domestic regulated input prices were lower than the inputs' market value. If there are no unregulated prices, or if such prices appear to be distorted by governmental price regulation, the export prices or other jurisdictions' market prices may serve as the benchmark. Under the US/EU proposal, benchmark data from that country's market or the world market could also be used to establish a subsidy indirectly benefiting an exporting industry, which operates downstream of the direct recipient of the subsidy. The US view was that natural gas dual pricing represented, "no difference between the government provision of a natural resource at less than fair market value and the government provision of a cash grant allowing the purchase of a natural resource at less than fair market value." Duane Layton, et al, Worldwide: Draft WTO Anti-Dumping and Subsidy Texts Released in Doha Round, Mayer Brown LLP, (Dec. 5, 2007); Subsidies Disciplines Requiring Clarification and Improvement, Communication from the United States, March 18, 2003. Available at http://www.ustr.gov/releases/2003/03/2003-03-18-wto-subsidies.PDF.

Any efforts to rely on a global price benchmark would likely fail to find that the Gulf States conferred a benefit. It is widely agreed that a global price for natural gas does not exist.[86] Because of the lack of an internationally agreed pricing framework, such as that which exists in the oil market, it would be inappropriate to apply a global benchmark in respect to the Gulf system. Globally, there are only regional natural gas prices in terms of pipeline export, and the nascent LNG spot market, at the time of writing, only comprises approximately 10 percent of the global gas trade.

If production costs were utilized as the benchmark, it would still be difficult to justify that a benefit had been conferred to domestic producers. The Gulf producers do not provide natural gas for domestic industries at less than adequate remuneration; rather, they provide the natural gas at the cost of production plus transportation.[87]

Therefore, since the administrative price is not below the cost of production, a WTO panel would likely not determine that the Gulf States provide natural gas at less than adequate remuneration.

---

[86] See, generally, Hossein Razavi , Natural Gas Pricing in the Countries of the Middle East and North Africa, The Energy Journal, July 2009.

[87] Id.

Chapter 5

PROHIBITED AND ACTIONABLE SUBSIDIES

Even if natural gas dual pricing meets the definition of a subsidy under Art. 1.1 of the ASCM, that finding does not immediately place it under WTO disciplines. Article 1.2 mandates that only *specific* subsidies-those limited to an enterprise or industry- are subject to the WTO disciplines; nonspecific subsidies are non-actionable.[88]

Specific subsidies fall into one of two classifications: prohibited or actionable. Two categories of subsidies are prohibited by Article 3 of the ASCM. The first category comprises subsidies contingent, de facto or de jure, whether wholly or as one of several conditions, on export performance (i.e., export subsidies). The second category comprises subsidies contingent, whether totally or as one of several other conditions, upon the use of domestic over imported goods (i.e., local content subsidies).[89] These subsidies are prohibited regardless of their effect. There is no need for a WTO Member to exhibit any injury or adverse effect on their domestic producers or its market, because the negative effects are presumed to exist.[90]

---

[88] Article 1.2 of the ASCM states that "a subsidy as defined in paragraph 1 shall be subject to the provisions of Part II [prohibited subsidies] or shall be subject to the provisions of Part III [actionable subsidies] or V [Countervailing Measures] only if such a subsidy is specific in accordance with the provisions of Article 2."

[89] Commentators have criticized the seemingly arbitrary line drawn between prohibited subsidies, which the ASCM concludes to be specific per se, and actionable subsidies, which must be shown to be specific. Critics of this legal bifurcation opined that the ASCM is ostensibly considering the overall export industry as a specific industry. The Law and Economics of Contingent Protection in the WTO, Edward Elgar Publishing, 2008. p. 350.

[90] Article 4.7 of the ASCM holds that if a subsidy is determined to be prohibited; the WTO Panel will recommend its immediate withdrawal. A WTO Member has several options when faced with an actionable subsidy. A WTO Member may apply a countervailing duty if subsidized

The second set of subsidies are those that are *actionable*, which are not prohibited *per se*, but may be liable to challenges if there are adverse effects on other Members.[91]

In the case of the Gulf States, their dual pricing framework does not fall under the first prong of the prohibited analysis, that is an export subsidy. There are numerous categories of industrial users who use the natural gas inputs for reasons other than export, for example, the public utility sector. Defining dual-pricing framework as import substitution subsidies-subsidies predicated on the utilization of domestic products over imported ones is also not relevant. The Gulf countries practiced a form of import-substitution policies in the 1960s and 1970s; however, in their bid to develop under export-led growth strategy, they liberalized many economic sectors and actively encourage participation of foreign multinationals, as well as import large volumes of Western capital equipment.

The dual pricing regime in the Gulf induces industrial end-users to utilize domestic natural gas, rather than imports. However, it stretches the intent and meaning of the ASCM to apply this to the Gulf dual pricing as an import substitution subsidy. The key term in the analysis is the contingency requirement in Article 3.1(b). Contingency is quite different in meaning from an inducement, and such an inducement fails to meet the necessary threshold to imply an import substitution subsidy. Article 3.1(b) states that the subsidy must be contingent "upon the use of domestic over imported goods." The term "contingent" has been interpreted by numerous WTO Panels as meaning, "dependent upon" or "conditional" on the use of domestic over imported goods.[92] The contingency requirement would only be met if the government provided the natural gas feedstock to a producer on the condition that it only uses domestic goods.

In the case of the Gulf, the contingency test is not met, as the utilization of natural gas is not predicated on other criteria. The Gulf dual pricing framework does not meet the standard enunciated by Article 3.1 (a) or (b) of the ASCM, and is therefore not a prohibited subsidy.

---

imports are causing a material damage to a domestic industry. Additionally, the Member has the option of bringing the issue before a WTO dispute settlement panel.

[91] In the GATT language, actionable subsidies cause "injury," "serious prejudice," or "nullification and impairment of benefits." Terence P. Stewart, The GATT Uruguay Round: a negotiating history (1986-1994), Kluwer Law International, 1999 pp.238-40.

[92] See Appellate Body Report, Canada-Aircraft , paras 162-80; Appellate Body Report, US-FSC, paras 96-121; Appellate Body Report, Canada-Autos, paras 95-117.

5.1. SPECIFICITY ANALYSIS: IS DUAL PRICING AN ACTIONABLE SUBSIDY?

As stated above, only subsidies, which are specific to certain enterprises, are subject to WTO disciplines of the ASCM, and only specific subsidies are subject to countervailing measures[93]

The ASCM defines three classes of specific subsidies:[94]

- Enterprise specificity. A government targets a particular company or companies for subsidization;
- Industry specificity. A government targets a particular sector or sectors for subsidization.
- Regional specificity. A government targets producers in specified parts of its territory for subsidization.

Article 2.1(b) provides that when the granting authority establishes objective criteria or conditions administering the provision of the subsidy, specificity does not exist if the conditions are strictly adhered to, and the eligibility is automatic granted. This article provides that if the eligibility is limited and based upon explicit, verifiable and neutral criteria, do not favor certain industries over other, and are essentially, applied horizontally, then specificity would not exist. In the Gulf, there is no such discrimination; low-cost natural gas feedstock is available to all industries and all companies, whether domestic or foreign.

In the case of the Gulf States, natural gas is not legislatively limited to certain industries, regions or enterprises; it is unconditionally made available to all end users. Therefore, the legislative threshold is not met by the Gulf States' dual pricing provision of natural gas. In regard to whether the Gulf States' *in fact* specifically incorporate specificity in their provision of natural gas, the most relevant provisions laid out by Article 2.1 will be applied, in particular, (a), (b) and (c).

---

[93] This phrase is from Article 1.2 of the ASCM. During the Uruguay Round insisted that this notion of specificity, which was already applied in US countervailing law prior to the implementation of the ASCM, be included in the Agreement. Petros C. Mavroidis, et al, The law and economics of contingent protection in the WTO, Edward Elgar Publishing, 2008. P. 350.

[94] The following list is supplied from the WTO Homepage, see World Trade Organization: Subsidies and Countervailing Measures Overview. Available at <http://www.wto.org/english/tratop_E/scm_e/subs_e.htm> .

Article 2.1(a) states that a de facto subsidy exists if it is in fact limited to a certain number of enterprises. The Gulf dual pricing scheme does not meet this requirement, as stated above, it is available throughout the economy and utilized by all sectors.

Article 2.1(b) states that while the subsidy may be available to all sectors certain sectors may overwhelmingly use the subsidized good, which would indicate specificity. Some industrial sectors in the Gulf utilize natural gas more than others, simply because different industrial and manufacturing methods utilize varying degrees of natural gas feedstock. For example, the petrochemical and power sectors both use disproportionately more gas than other industrial sectors,[95] therefore, under the ASCM, the disproportionate sectoral use would weigh heavily for a specificity determination.

However, varying degrees of natural gas usage may not be enough to imply de facto specificity. In *US-Softwood Lumber IV*, the Panel analyzed the Canadian lumber program and determined that while Canada argued that the timber was available to all comers, inherently, due to the intrinsic attributes of the good, the stumpage could only be utilized by certain industries.[96]

Article 2.1(c), which holds that specificity applies when there is "the granting of disproportionately large amounts of subsidy to certain enterprises," does not prima facie apply to the Gulf countries. The Gulf countries tend to be overly prejudiced under this analysis as they are newly industrializing and as such, have little economic diversification. By virtue of being in the beginning stages of economic modernization, by default, there are limited industries that would benefit from the natural gas. Nonetheless, there are enough industries in the Gulf countries, steel smelting, fertilizers, petrochemical industries, and the power sector that Article 2.1(C) would not apply.

If a large group of industries are able to utilize the subsidy, albeit in varying degrees, it cannot be held as specific under Article 2.1 of the ASCM. Gulf gas is available to all industrial sectors and all end-users at an equivalent low-price; it is more akin to roads, general infrastructure projects, or low-interest loans granted without bias by the government. Because the actual and potential end-users are spread out throughout many economic sectors, the Gulf natural gas dual pricing does not meet the specificity requirements in Article 2.1 of the ASCM.

---

[95] N.S. Maina, Development of Petrochemicals from Natural Gas (Methane), ChemClass Journal, Vol. 2 (2005) pp.25-31.
[96] US-Softwood Lumber IV, Panel Report, para. 7.116.

Chapter 6

CONCLUSION

Under the requirements of the ASCM, the Gulf dual price natural gas framework would likely not be considered WTO inconsistent. The above analysis demonstrated that even if the dual pricing system were considered a subsidy, it would not come within the ambit of ASCM and would not be prohibited or actionable under the ASCM. The allegation emanating from many Western petrochemical firms that Gulf natural gas dual pricing is against the WTO principles and grants an unfair competitive advantage to Gulf petrochemical firms does not have a sufficient legal foundation under the WTO rules.

Furthermore, Gulf countries consider the natural gas sector and their industrialization plans which depend upon it, to be of the utmost national priority. Through dual pricing and provision of inexpensive natural gas, they seek to develop a robust industrial sector, and built upon the provision of inexpensive natural gas. Through the construction of an industrial sector, the Gulf countries hope to initiate economic diversification that would be able to move them away from their dependence on unprocessed hydrocarbon export. While there are undisputed benefits for the Gulf States to join the WTO, the concern does exist that by joining it they may constrain their future opportunities for sustainable development of their countries and economies. Nonetheless, because of the GCC's focus on export-led growth, the benefits of joining the WTO outweigh the negatives.

Dual pricing of natural gas has led to some negative externalities, such as extremely high growth in natural gas, and electricity demand rates. These growth rates have caused the Gulf States to have an extremely large carbon footprint and environmental damage. It is important that in attempting to develop their economies, Gulf policymakers balance the need to deliver economic opportunities to their citizens, but it should not be at the cost of equity for future generations. Moreover, while a global rules-based regime such as the WTO is needed to ensure the smooth running of the global economy, it should not be at the expense of the development of the Gulf. The Gulf countries are well within their rights to industrialize by leveraging their prodigious natural gas resources into sustainable economic growth. The conflict over dual pricing policies is likely to intensify in the future as Western petrochemical firms fail to compete with Gulf-based ones; however, as the prior analysis illustrated, dual pricing of natural gas by the Gulf States is not WTO-inconsistent. Dual pricing should be considered a viable industrial policy for other energy-rich developing nations in their drive to create self-sustaining economic growth.

INDEX